Redemption and Relationship

Wycliffe Studies in Gospel, Church, and Culture

The series entitled Wycliffe College Studies in Gospel, Church, and Culture is intended to present topical subject matter in an accessible form and seeks to appeal to a broad audience. Typically titles in the series derive from sermons given by the faculty of Wycliffe College, Toronto, in its Founders' Chapel. The current volume on the Book of Exodus is the third in the series and derives from a sermon series given in the winter of 2017.

Redemption and Relationship

Meditations on Exodus

EDITED BY
Andrew C. Witt

WIPF & STOCK · Eugene, Oregon

REDEMPTION AND RELATIONSHIP
Meditations on Exodus
Wycliffe Studies in Gospel, Church, and Culture

Copyright © 2018 Andrew C. Witt. All rights reserved. Except for brief quotations in critical publications or reviews, no part of this book may be reproduced in any manner without prior written permission from the publisher. Write: Permissions, Wipf and Stock Publishers, 199 W. 8th Ave., Suite 3, Eugene, OR 97401.

Wipf & Stock
An Imprint of Wipf and Stock Publishers
199 W. 8th Ave., Suite 3
Eugene, OR 97401

www.wipfandstock.com

PAPERBACK ISBN: 978-1-5326-4017-9
HARDCOVER ISBN: 978-1-5326-4018-6
EBOOK ISBN: 978-1-5326-4019-3

Manufactured in the U.S.A.

Contents

Introduction | vii
—Andrew C. Witt

1 The Surprising Beginning of God's Plan to Rescue His People | 1
—Marion Taylor

2 His Life as He Knew It Was Over | 8
—L. Ann Jervis

3 Divine Naming | 13
—Ephraim Radner

4 The Theatre of God's Power | 19
—Stephen G. W. Andrews

5 From Bitterness to Joy: Lessons in the Wilderness School | 25
—Thomas Power

6 This is the Word of the Lord | 31
—Catherine Sider-Hamilton

7 Ours is the Battle, Christ is the Victory | 38
—J. Glen Taylor

Contents

8   God's Gift of Days and Life | 46
    —Annette Brownlee

9   Moses' Intercession for Israel, and How It Helps Us Understand the Cross | 51
    —Alan L. Hayes

10 The Full Exodus Story | 59
    —Peter Robinson

Bibliography | 65

List of Contributors | 67

Introduction

ANDREW C. WITT

EVERY READER COMES TO the book of Exodus with preconceived notions of the stories being told there. Some may come having heard them in their childhood, perhaps in a Sunday school class: the baby Moses placed in a reed basket in the River Nile; the adult Moses' encounter with God at the burning bush; Pharaoh and the plagues of Egypt; the miraculous parting of the Red Sea and the people of Israel walking through on dry land; the volcanic atmosphere of God's appearing on Mount Sinai; the disobedience of Israel with the golden calf; the revelation of God to Moses from the cleft of a rock; and the glory of God descending on the tabernacle. From youth, their understanding of God (and maybe your own) was shaped by these ancient and otherworldly tales of a people and the God who saved them from the oppressive Egyptians. Others, like me, encountered the book later in life. My own reading of the book was filtered through the story of Jesus in the Gospels, and I had a whole other set of questions. How is this story from the Old Testament related to the gospel story of Jesus' death and resurrection? How can I hold these two stories together, or should I even hold them together? What do they teach me about the God who created the world, the God who rescued me, and the God who calls me into new life? Whether you are coming to this book of meditations on Exodus having heard these stories your whole life, or only recently, or perhaps somewhere in between, we all come to the book of Exodus in our own ways, with our own experiences, and likely our own expectations of what we will find.

The same has also been true of the different communities with which we identify ourselves. The Christian tradition comes to the book shaped by the name we give it: Exodus. This title comes from the early Greek translation of the Old Testament (the Septuagint) and highlights one of the main events of the whole Old Testament story: the salvation of Israel from slavery under the Egyptians. The title is a fitting entryway into the book. It reminds readers of the earlier deliverance of Abram and Sarai from the famine which took them to Egypt (Gen 12–13), a story which prefigures the later history of their descendants. It is also the story which grounds the covenant God makes with his people in Exodus 19–24, "I am Yhwh your God, who brought you out of the land of Egypt, out of the house of slavery" (Exod 20:2). The exodus from Egypt is likewise the story which Moses appeals to after Israel's terrible sin with the golden calf: "O Yhwh, why does your wrath burn hot against your people, whom you brought out of the land of Egypt with great power and a mighty hand?" (Exod 32:11). It is a story, then, which grounds Israel's relationship with her God. Its foundational place in the mind of ancient Israel would allow its figure to be picked up even later as Israel struggled to understand its experience of exile in the hands of the Assyrians and Babylonians. Just

INTRODUCTION

as that first generation, YHWH would lead the people out of exile and back into the Promised Land in a new exodus with a new Moses, the Servant of YHWH (Isa 40–55). The exodus of the Israelites, then, plays a profound role in how God's people have understood their relationship to him. One contemporary Christian theologian has even gone so far as to hold the story of Israel's "resurrection" from Egypt together with the resurrection of Jesus, identifying the Creator God by them: "God is whoever raised Jesus from the dead, having before raised Israel from Egypt."[1]

Unlike Christian tradition, the name of the book in Jewish tradition does not come from the main events of the story but from the opening words of the book, w^e'*ēlleh* $š^e$*môt*, or "And these are the names" (1:1). This title has different connotations than in Christian tradition, but it introduces the book with similar theological depth. By beginning with the word "and" (w^e), the title reminds us that the stories we are about to read do not stand on their own, but are a continuation of the story from the previous book of Genesis (or in Hebrew $b^e r\bar{e}$'*šît*, "In the beginning"). It also reminds us that that story, while beginning with the creation of the universe, had narrowed its vision to Abraham's descendants, through whom God had promised to bring blessing to every family on earth (Gen 12:3). "These are the names." The names listed here are the names of the "sons of Israel" ($b^e n\hat{e}$ *yiśrā'ēl*) who have grown in the centuries since Jacob led them to Egypt. As we are told, the seventy of Jacob's family have multiplied and grown strong, filling up the land (Exod 1:5–7, recalling the divine blessing of Gen 1:28). There is, then, a sense of anticipation as one enters into the book of "names"—this is not any old story, but one in which God is personally involved

1. Jenson, *Systematic Theology*, 63.

Introduction

with particular people, people like us, people with names, people with a story, with a history. Given the account of their ancestors in the book of Genesis, it is unsurprising that their own experience with Yhwh would bring numerous threats to the blessing they would provide to the world, both from outside their people and within.

The title in Jewish tradition also contains a deeper meaning when we consider the most important *name* revealed in the book, God's own name, Yhwh. While we know from Genesis that the name itself was known before Moses' encounter with God at the burning bush (Gen 4:26; 12:8; 13:4; 15:7; 21:33; 24:31, 48; 26:25; 28:13; 49:18), the story of the exodus provided a theological depth to this name which was unknown beforehand. As John Sailhamer has noted, Moses' question about God's name in Exodus 3 was concerned with more than just God's identity: "He was asking a question about the very nature of God."[2] Indeed, as Wycliffe's own research professor Christopher Seitz has argued, "God's name is the most personal revelation of God's own character, and as such is not a proper name in the strict sense (like Jim or Sally), but a name appropriate to God's character as God."[3] While the giving of the name in Exodus 3 and 6 has thematic links to the presence of God and the glory or power of God, it is in the exodus itself that Yhwh demonstrates the nature which undergirds his name. Seitz goes on to write, "[The] Israelites in Egypt, Moses, Aaron, Pharaoh, and all his hosts might well know the name of God, but they have yet to know who God wishes to reveal himself as. That will be made manifest in the deliverance of his people and the destruction of those who oppose that deliverance. 'He is who he

---

2. Sailhamer, *Pentateuch as Narrative*, 246.
3. Seitz, *Word Without End*, 239.

is' in these events and as such makes himself known—fully rather than for the first time—as Yhwh."[4]

Whether one prefers to call the book "Exodus" or "And these are the names," the stories told therein—and the Name which we learn—hold together two aspects which connect Israel with her God: redemption and relationship. The title of this book attempts to hold these twin themes together. In the book of Exodus the reader is not only given an answer about the identity of the God of Israel—I am who I am—but a narrative which explains that identity by recounting Israel's experience of Yhwh in the deserts of ancient Egypt. The divine name, then, tells us something about the character of the God of creation, and his actions to defend and rescue Israel tell us something about his purposes and plans in his world. In the following meditations, the faculty of Wycliffe College catch a glimpse of the God of our two-testament witness—with face covered and even then only seeing his back—the One who "raised Jesus from the dead, having before raised Israel from Egypt."

---

4. Ibid., 243–44.

1

The Surprising Beginning of God's Plan to Rescue His People

Marion Taylor

The book of Exodus is a book which tells the story of the deliverance of God's people from Egypt. It opens with the names of Joseph's brothers who joined him in Egypt during a time of famine. It then adds a brief but significant note about the deaths of Joseph, his brothers, and their families. The descendants of Jacob continued to increase in number rapidly—they were no longer a single family but the beginning of a nation; and so the narrator says, "the land was filled with the descendants of Jacob." The increase of Jacob's descendants was a mark of the beginning of the fulfillment of the promise given to Abraham and then to Isaac and Jacob—that God would bless Abraham and his seed and make them a great nation. Another of the promises given to the patriarchs was the blessing of land; and, as the narrator of Exodus 1 makes very clear, one of the problems faced by the growing nation of Israel was that God's people were now in Egypt outside the land of promise.

What made things even worse was that the new pharaoh did not remember Joseph and all he had done for

Egypt. He not only viewed the presence of non-Egyptians as a political threat but he was particularly threatened by the growing numbers of Israelites. So instead of expelling the Israelites from Egypt, he essentially enslaved them, forcing them to build cities that would store his wealth. When the pharaoh's initial plan to stop the population growth through oppression did not work, he invoked harsher methods. The Egyptian pharaoh—whose name we do not know—ordered two named midwives to kill male Hebrew babies as soon as they were born. But even this plan failed because Shiphrah and Puah feared God, and let the baby boys live. When confronted by the pharaoh, these courageous women lied, claiming that Hebrew women were more vigorous than Egyptian women as they gave birth before the midwives arrived (1:17–19). For their courage in standing up to the pharaoh and for their ingenuity in coming up with a plan to save the lives of Hebrew babies, God blessed Shiphrah and Puah. The pharaoh came up with yet another genocidal plan: throwing the babies into the Nile.

It is at this point in the story that the narrator's focus narrows and draws us into the lives of one of the families impacted by the pharaoh's genocidal decree. To parents from the house of Levi, a beautiful son was born. Later in the story we find out the names of these parents. The name of the father of Moses was Amram, which likely means "exalted people." His mother's name, Jochebed, similarly suggests that she was a woman of faith: "Yahweh is glorious" or "Yahweh is her glory." Jochebed is one of a handful of women who play a critical role in this important episode of the story of God's deliverance of the Israelites from Egypt. Her name has fascinated interpreters because she is the first person in Scripture to have a name that includes the shortened form of the name Yahweh ("Yah"), the name later revealed to her son Moses at the burning bush. Scottish commentator Alexander Whyte speaks for many when he says:

> It is very tantalizing to be told her remarkable name and to be told no more. Was *God thy-glory* the remarkable name that Moses gave to his mother as often as he looked back at all that he owed to her, and as often as he rose up and called her blessed? Or was her very remarkable name her own invention? Was her striking name her own seal that she had set to her own vow which she made to her own God after some great grace and goodness of her own God? Or,—again did the angel of the Lord visit that daughter of the house of Levi on some Jabbok-like or Annunciation-night, and so name her as the sun rose upon her prayer?[1]

These tantalizing suggestions at the very least should draw attention to the role Moses' mother plays in this story. When baby Moses reached the age when most babies become more active, sleep less, and are more vocal, his mother hid him in an ark-like wicker basket sealed with pitch in the reeds by the bank of the Nile. Although her motives and plan are not fleshed out, Moses' mother hoped that her beautiful child would be rescued by a sympathetic Egyptian. She may even have hoped that he would be rescued by the Egyptian princess who would have had the resources to give her child everything she could not. It was likely Jochebed who instructed her daughter Miriam to watch over the baby from afar, and it was probably her idea that Miriam offer to find a wet nurse for the child.

---

1. Whyte, *Bible Characters*, 239.

Although Moses' mother was most likely the one who had come up with the elaborate plan to save her child, some interpreters suggest that Miriam did much more than follow her mother's instructions. Phyllis Trible, for example, notes that Miriam took "initiative to shape the destiny of the child"; by speaking to Pharaoh's daughter, she "shape[d] the future by defining the need of Pharaoh's daughter."[2] Indeed, "her words propose a perfect arrangement" and effectively brought Pharaoh's daughter and the baby's mother together. Whether the brilliant plan to have Moses' mother nurse her own child was Jochebed's or Miriam's is not as important as the acknowledgment that the plan worked and baby Moses was rescued by the daughter of the pharaoh who had mandated the death of Hebrew baby boys. In one final ironic turn, Moses' very own mother was paid to nurse her own son until he was old enough to be brought back to the pharaoh's daughter, who became his adoptive mother.

What should be made of this detailed story of the birth and rescue of the one called to be Israel's deliverer that begins the larger drama of the Exodus? Five women are involved in saving the child whom God later called to deliver God's people from Egypt: two named midwives, Shiphrah and Puah; Moses' mother and sister, Jochebed and Miriam (who goes on to play a significant role in leadership together with her brothers Moses and Aaron); and finally, the Egyptian princess. On the surface of things, the Hebrew women had little in common with the Egyptian princess; the Hebrew midwives and the baby's mother and sister were oppressed Hebrews enslaved by the genocidal pharaoh whose daughter was a privileged royal woman.

---

2. Trible, "Bringing Miriam Out of the Shadows," 16.

But together these women planned and risked their lives to bring life when the pharaoh had ordered death.

This story is one of many stories in Scripture about women that are placed at the beginning of God's initiation of a new work with his people. We see this fronting not only in the exodus story, but in the story of conquest where the first gentile convert Rahab confessed, "I know that the Lord has given you the land and that terror of you has fallen on us, and that all the inhabitants of the land have melted away before you" (Josh 2:9). We see the fronting of stories of women in the transition to monarchy with the story of Ruth (whose descendant was King David), and in the story of Hannah (whose son Samuel had a critical role in the transition to monarchy). Later we see the fronting of a story about women in the book of Esther, where Esther saves God's people from genocide. And, of course, in the New Testament we see the fronting of stories of women in the annunciation, birth, death, and resurrection of Jesus. The fronting of the stories of women in larger narratives where women's lives are not featured makes feminists like Cheryl Exum angry. Exum claims that women in the Exodus story are used to produce the deliverer, and then drop off the page. But is this the role women play in the narrative? The women featured in the birth story of Moses, like those featured in many other narratives, are a consistent reminder that women have an essential role to play in the story of salvation. Both women and men were integral to the story of God even though their roles in that story are not always acknowledged in the Old Testament.

The opening chapter of Exodus does more than raise issues related to gender, outsiders, the marginalized, and the enslaved. The story gives witness to the ways God uses faithful yet seemingly insignificant women and men, outsiders, the marginalized and enslaved, as part of his bigger plan of salvation. The Hebrew midwives lied and refused to obey the pharaoh because they knew killing babies was wrong. Although Moses' parents recognized that he was a beautiful child, they did not know what God had in store for his life as deliverer and lawgiver and friend of God. Moses' family risked all because they knew that the life was precious and worth risking all to save. God also used an Egyptian princess as part of the plan to save Moses, a plan whose benefits included—as the Book of Acts suggests—Moses being "educated in all the wisdom of the Egyptians" (Acts 7:22).

In the following lessons through the book of Exodus, God's plan to redeem his people from slavery in Egypt will gradually unfold, a plan that included the actions of seemingly insignificant midwives and courageous family members who lived their lives in faithful obedience to the God of Israel who brings life not death. May we remember that the same Lord God who delivered his people from oppression is the same God who sent his son Jesus to fulfill what was promised and awaited by Israel, and to accomplish that decisive event of deliverance and salvation once for all.

Scripture: Exodus 1:18–2:10.

Questions for Further Reflection:

1. Looking back over the story of your own faith journey, who were the women and men involved that gave that story shape?
2. Take the time to give God thanks for those people, and perhaps the surprising role they may have

played in helping you through difficult experiences along the way.

3. How might God have been using them in the larger story of your life?

2

His Life as He Knew It Was Over

L. Ann Jervis

THIS IS ONE OF the great theophanies of the Bible, one of the great presentations of God revealing Godself. And, as in many of the Bible's theophanies, when God reveals Godself it is not just a revelation of who God is: it is a revelation of who the recipient is. Perhaps better put, it is a revelation of who the recipient is in God's sight. And this may have been why Moses' first response to God's introduction of Godself out of the burning bush was fear. Moses hid his face, for he was afraid to look at God.

This seems like a very natural instinct. Now it may be that somehow Moses, even though he had been raised as an Egyptian prince, knew that the custom of the Hebrew people was to hide one's face from God. After all, he identified enough with the Hebrew people that he killed an Egyptian he saw beating one of them. But Moses' instinct to hide from God's self-revelation—to hide from God's unexpected and unbidden self-presentation—may also have been an instinctive recognition that this was going somewhere, that this truly remarkable happening was not going to be over when God decided to go back to God's normally hidden and distant place. Moses' fear was quite rightly a fear for his life. He instinctively knew that when God spoke to him, his life as he knew it was over.

The narrator gently sets the scene. Moses, who has now settled in Midian after fleeing Egypt because the news of his murder of the Egyptian was out, is shepherding his father-in-law's flock. The narrator says that, in the course of shepherding, Moses had "led his flock beyond the wilderness and had come to Horeb, the mountain of God." The story of what will be Moses' life after God's self-revelation is here foreshadowed in a few words. The course of Moses' life—the immense struggles and challenges and privileges—are compressed in the narrator's setting of the scene. As a result of the theophany Moses is about to receive, Moses will indeed be a shepherd leading his flock beyond the wilderness, and he will come to the mountain of God.

After Moses is on the mountain of God, without preparation the angel of the Lord appears to Moses in a flame of fire out of a bush. Moses is astonished that the bush can be on fire but not be burned up. He focuses intensely on the bush; and once God has Moses' entire attention, God speaks to Moses out of the bush, calling Moses' name twice.

At first Moses seems quite fine with responding to this amazing moment, speaking back, "Here am I." But then God expands God's revelation of who God is. God is so holy that Moses should not come any closer to the burning bush; God is so holy that even where he is standing is holy ground and he must take off his sandals. And God tells Moses that, though God is so holy that Moses must keep away, at the same time God is the God of Moses' own father, Amram. And God is the God of the fathers of Israel: of Abraham, of Isaac, and of Jacob.

It is at this point that Moses hides his face and is afraid to look at God. Moses may have known what happened at least to Abraham when God appeared to him. Abraham's life as he knew it was over. Moses certainly knew that his father Amram had had a very hard life. Shortly after Moses was born Amram had to allow his wife to hide him in a basket in the Nile in order to protect him from the pharaoh's hatred of the Hebrews. Moses knew that this God who was revealing himself was not going to offer him an easy life. But God doesn't stop talking to Moses when Moses hides his face. God goes on and declares God's intention to deliver God's people from the oppression of the Egyptians: "I have come down to deliver them from the Egyptians, and to bring them up out of that land to a good and broad land."

And then comes the part that Moses may have instinctively feared: "I will send you." God says, "I will send you to Pharaoh to bring my people, the Israelites, out of Egypt."

Moses' response is: "Who am I?" This is a very different response than his first one: "Here I am." Now Moses recognizes that even though he has tried to hide from God, his identity has nevertheless changed by virtue of God's self-revelation. *Who am I now?* may be what Moses is really saying: "I am no longer a simple shepherd in Midian trying to have a normal life—even though my life so far has been complicated." *Who am I NOW?* "Who am I now that you, God, would have me go to the one I have escaped from—to Pharaoh—and ask him to let my people go? Who do you think I am? Who do *I* think I am?" God's answer is, "I will be with you." This is now Moses' identity. Moses is now the man whose life is taken over by God and God's will. In response to Moses' question—who am I?—God says, "You are *God is with me*—that is who you are."

The theophany that Moses received was, of course, astoundingly remarkable; and it has become foundational for both Judaism and Christianity. But have not many of us also received theophanies? Perhaps much humbler, but each of us has heard God call our name in one way or another; each of us have recognized that that call means our lives are no longer ours (as if they ever were). We have recognized that we can no longer say, "Here I am." Because God has called out to us, and because we have responded, we know that who we are is "God is with me/God is with us."

This means for us, as it did for Moses, that the work of our lives is now God's work for deliverance and justice. May this passage encourage us to remember and give thanks that God has called out to us; and may we be able to set the work of this day in the context of gratitude that we have been given the identity "God is with you."

Scripture: Exodus 3:1–12

Questions for Further Reflection:

1. Have you ever had your own encounter with God? What was your experience like, and how did it affect you?

2. The meditation helps us to see that God's presence has become an important part of Moses' own identity. In what ways has God made his presence known in your life? Are there any moments you can recall in which God has called out to you?

Redemption and Relationship

3. How might God's presence, made known to Moses and revealed to us in Christ, give us hope and encouragement as we journey on in our days, weeks, and years?

3

Divine Naming

Ephraim Radner

Exodus is a story. It has people in it; actions, places, developing and concluding events, directions, limits . . . names. Exodus—like all the Bible—is a heavenly map, a transcendent travel guide, an eternal law code, an ethereal building manual, a divine telephone book. The book of Exodus, however, also contains one of the most offensive texts in the Bible: the revelation of God's name.

> God said to Moses, "I AM WHO I AM." And he said, "Say this to the people of Israel, 'I AM has sent me to you.'" God also said to Moses, "Say this to the people of Israel, 'The LORD, the God of your fathers, the God of Abraham, the God of Isaac, and the God of Jacob, has sent me to you': this is my name for ever, and thus I am to be remembered throughout all generations. (Exod 3:14–15 RSV)

"I am who I am." There is no problem for the modern critic here. That name is just fine: "being" itself, all that is, wide, open, embracive. There's a God for you! The eighteenth-century Deists were happy with this name. They even suggested that Moses got it first from the Egyptians. There was an inscription to the Egyptian goddess Isis, recorded by Plutarch and Proclus in antique times, which says that she is "all that is, was, and will be." Moses, the Deists said, simply recognized the deepest truth of all ancient wisdom: God is the "all." And that is good.

It's the second part of God's name they bristled at: the Lord, the God of your fathers, of Abraham, Isaac, Jacob . . . and of this finally cramped and vitriolic old man named Moses. How dare one insist that, just here, to this man, in this place named Horeb, and for this people named Israel—how dare God, who is "all in all"—give a name and do a deed unknown to other people and unexperienced by other nations. As is known, the eighteenth-century Deists are notable for articulating a rising hatred against the Jews for just this reason, and against normal Christians who built upon it. Orthodox or evangelical Christians, who embraced the Old Testament, the Deists called "rabbinic"—a dirty word to modernity, still to this day bound to be perceived as arrogance—God "for us," us. Bigotry!

So there's a deep hostility to divine electing particularity in this era, and it's bound up to the anti-Judaic and finally anti-Semitic cast of modernity as a whole. So goes the rhyme: "How odd of God to choose the Jews." It was coined by the British journalist (and as it turned out later, Soviet spy) William Ewer. Odd of God to choose the Jews, but not choose the Chinese or the Turks or the Indians or finally the Germans and the Russians. A reasonable religion, a natural one, an acceptable liberal faith, the philosopher Lessing wrote, will move from the narrow and self-centered concerns of the Jews—primitively infantile—to the wider Gentile-tolerating Christians—adolescent—and finally to a universal morality of love. Adult faith.[1] One big name for all.

Yet there is Pascal, whose private prayer, sewn into the lining of his coat, has become the great challenge to such a modern religion: "Fire. God of Abraham, God of Isaac, God of Jacob. Not of philosophers and scholars. Certainty, certainty, heartfelt, joy, Peace. God of Jesus Christ . . ." Without the God of Abraham, Isaac, and Jacob—the God of the living, as Jesus says (Matt 22:32)—there is, Pascal insists, no light, no joy, no here, no now; no calling; no demands; no desires; no repentance; no mercy. Not without the God of the Jews, of Abraham, Isaac, and Jacob. Pascal is right, of course; and the philosophers of modernity are wrong.

See what God does in this text from Exodus, beginning at the start of chapter three: God "sees" the affliction and oppression of his people; God "hears" their cries; God "comes down" to deliver them; God "visits" the Israelites; God "brings them up"; God "stretches out his hand"; God "smites" the Egyptians; God "does wonders"; God "gives favor." God does this here, at this time, to this one and that one, to this people and that.

"I am who I am," God tells Moses; yet this is what my name does—all this, to this person, and that person. For God's name is about our names, because his name is word and work together. Those who argue on the basis of both Hebrew syntax and theological coherence for the causative mode of the divine name's verbal form—that is, those who argue that the creative character of God's being is bound up in the name "Yahweh"—are surely right. "I am who I am" means I do what I do; I cause to be what will be. God speaks and it is . . . just this. He acts because he has a name

---

1. See his *Education of the Human Race*.

and he names. "God said, 'Let there be light,' and there was light . . . and God called the light 'Day'" (Gen 1:3, 5). He did not call it *night*; he called it *day*, and so it is. And so you are who you are. The whole world of particulars is His, and God orders them particularly. Not just in Genesis, but now Israel and Egypt. And now . . . even now.

God is the God of Joseph—suffering, successful, forgotten. He is his God. God is the God of Pharaoh, the forgetter of Joseph—cruel, tyrannical, grieving, feckless, blotted out. He is his God too, however unacknowledged. He is the God of Shiphrah and Puah, midwives to the Hebrews, courageous, common, commemorated. He is their God. He is the God of Moses, the God of Aaron, of Miriam, of Zipporah and Gershom, the God of Jethro and the family of Levi, driving their times forward, through generations, songs, failures, revivals. He is their God. He is the God of the Nile, of the sea, of deserts and mountains, of Sinai and Paran; the God of the manna, the God of the quails, the God of Law, the God of Torah, the God of "thou shalt" and of "thou shalt not," of Sabbath and of festival, of judgment and promise. He is all their God.

Take it away, and all of it disappears.

Contemporary society, of course, is filled with particulars, a plethora of things, but none of them have any organizing meaning. They have instead settled into a buzz, a haze, a gas-like distant dying star—things without a God who names them. But this God, who is the God of names (his name and our names), the God of stars whom he names one by one (Ps 147:4), the God of Abraham, Isaac, Jacob and Moses—he is Rahab's God, she who, having given away her body to strangers, gave her heart to Israel; he is Ahab's God, whose very heart rebelled against him, yet just there encountered the truth; he is Elizabeth's God, who gave away her son to prison and death; and Andrew's, who gave away his nets to follow Yeshua, Jesus. He is also the God of popes and martyrs; of widows and peasants; of slaves, tyrants, soldiers, and children: he is your God.

Why else is anyone here? Because all have been given a name. And all have names because God has a name, and his name is the name that is spoken and thus creates, such that "I am" becomes, and must become, "you are." Do not let anybody in this culture of clouded concoctions tell you that there are no particularities with a purpose—not philosophers, scholars, politicians, or whacky bishops. Go ahead, pray for the empty parking space, by all means, despite the scoffers; God has named it before you turned the engine on. Mind you, there are better names to put upon your lips—but they will be names nonetheless, whether of your neighbor, or of the holy servant down the street, or the secret sin or joy you bring to each of them. Life is a name, a person, and a place. This is not about sentimental, individual pietism either; it is the basis of social justice, of the transformation of persons, the renewal of communities. God knows the name of every star in the heavens, of every bird in the mountains (Ps 50:11), of every fetus in the womb (Ps 139:16), every tear from your eye (Ps 56:8), every hair on your head (Luke 12:7), every cell in your body, every life and death in his book (Rev 20:12). Our concern for this world, for one another, for ourselves, our prayers and acts on their behalf, is but a pale reflection of the miraculous naming of God. For salvation—joy and light—is about a name and about names as well. How odd of God to choose the Jews. When Ewer wrote this, an anonymous reply was quickly published, "God's not so odd; his Son is one." That is the God of Jesus Christ, before whose name every knee shall bow, everything in heaven, in earth, and

Redemption and Relationship

under the earth (Phil 2:10)—may he be praised forever and ever.

Scripture: Exodus 3:13–22

Questions for Further Reflection:

1. We do not usually think about the name of God as offensive, but in what ways does the meditation help us to see how the divine name might confront us?

2. Even so, the naming of particular things in God's creation gives those things purpose, and so, names are important. Does it comfort or surprise you that God not only has given you a name, but also knows your name? How does that affect the way you think about the purpose given to you within God's world?

4

The Theatre of God's Power

Stephen G. W. Andrews

> "But, Lord," Moses protested, "I have never been a man of ready speech, never in my life, not even now that you have spoken to me; I am slow and hesitant" (Exod 4:10, REB).

IN THE PREVIOUS REFLECTION, Ephraim Radner meditated on how the God of creation is a particular God, with a selective and exclusive interest in the oddest things of this world—not just the Jews, but you and me too. "All have names because God has a name," Ephraim exclaimed, "and his name is the name that is spoken and thus creates, such that *I am* becomes, and must become, *you are*." Such a reminder brings with it a renewed sense of awe that in his grand, universal design, nothing is insignificant to God: each of us has been included in his purposes, and he has given each of us a name that is hidden in the Name that is above every name.

But it is a remarkable thing how such a sense of privilege can also be experienced as a burden. God has, indeed, given me a name. But yesterday I found myself wishing that he had not given me either a name or an address, as I received a couple of caustic and confrontational letters from individuals who wanted to take issue with a presentation I recently gave. The hard truth is that when we respond to God, when we take upon ourselves the name that God has given us, we also take on a measure of responsibility. When we received our identity in Christ through baptism, we also received a duty to resist the world, the flesh, and the devil. When we enlisted as followers of Jesus Christ, we were given a commission to "go and make disciples" (Matt 28:19). These are great and noble purposes, to be sure. But they can fill us with anxiety and dread, the very antithesis of the gratitude grace is meant to arouse. Indeed, when we come to terms with the magnitude of what is being asked of us, we may well resonate with Moses when, having received his commission, he pleaded, "Lord, send anyone else you like" (v. 13).

One of the things that makes Moses easy to relate to is that he is a reluctant figure. It is worth commenting that, although the Bible exalts Moses as Israel's prophetic hero who dispenses the divine Law, its portrayal of his leadership does not gloss over his weaknesses. One Old Testament scholar writes, "One would expect the traditions about a founder of a nation to be embossed with legend and hyperbole. Yet what surprises about Moses . . . is his all-too-human, flesh-and-blood character." In fact, we have encountered his "all-too-human" reluctance before this. To God's bidding in chapter three, "Come, I shall send you to Pharaoh, and you are to bring my people Israel out of Egypt," Moses replies, "But who am I, that I should approach Pharaoh and that I should bring the Israelites out of Egypt?" (vv. 10–11).

Now, it is hard to know what was at the root of Moses' qualms, just as we are not always sure about what gives rise to our own diffidence and timidity. Was he looking for an easy way out? Did the prospect of having to face the ruler of one of the ancient Near East's most powerful nations fill him with dread? Had he witnessed enough trauma in his life and therefore wanted to be left alone to tend to his father-in-law's flock? His various responses to God indicate that he felt inadequate to the task, lacking both stature among the Israelites and the eloquence required to address a king. He claims that the Israelites simply would not believe him, and that his speech is muddled and inarticulate, owing in part to an impediment, a "heavy tongue," as the text says (*kᵉbad lāšôn*). It is not plain if this meant he struggled in the languages of the Hebrews or the Egyptian court, or if he just had trouble talking.

In believing that Moses had a speech defect, the Church Fathers and Rabbinic scholars were generally of a mind to see Moses' reluctance as an expression of his humility. He felt that he was incapable and therefore unworthy of speaking the words of God. And it is easy to read Moses' lack of self-confidence as characteristic of other biblical figures who received a prophetic calling. When summoned by God to speak, for instance, Jeremiah replied, "Ah! Lord God, I am not skilled in speaking; I am too young" (Jer 1:6). But whether Moses was making excuses or registering a legitimate concern, it is God's response that reframes the situation. For this story is not, in the end, about Moses and his motives and abilities. It is about God and his redemptive purposes in the world. "Who is it that gives man speech?" demands God. "Who makes him dumb or deaf? Who makes him keen-sighted or blind? Is it not I, the Lord?" (Exod 4: 11–12).

The principle here is that the theatre of God's power is human weakness and shortcoming. We can see how this principle works naturally. For example, Winston Churchill had a serious speech impediment. At the age of twenty-three he sought medical help because he was not able to pronounce the letter "s" properly. It is a problem that appears to have been genetic, since his father had a similar difficulty. He tried to remedy the defect by practicing tongue-twisters, such as, "The Spanish ships I cannot see for they are not in sight." In the end, he was not able to rid his speech of the mispronunciation, but by crafting his addresses carefully to avoid words that began or ended in an "s," and through varying his cadence and employing hesitation, he was able to use his handicap to great effect. He was finally able to say, "My impediment is no hindrance."

If such an effect is achievable by dint of human effort, how much more noteworthy is it if it comes by the hand of God. Indeed, this principle that God chooses the feeble and powerless in order to demonstrate his strength and sufficiency is at the heart of the gospel. Jesus is often in the company of the blind, the deaf, the sick, the leprous, and the demon possessed, while in his passion he himself takes on the role of the Suffering Servant. The apostle Paul's theology of the cross is thus fixed on the notion that God's "power is made perfect in weakness" (2 Cor 12:9). He writes, "But God chose what is foolish in the world to shame the wise; God chose what is weak in the world to shame the strong; God chose what is low and despised in the world, things that are not, to reduce to nothing things that are" (1 Cor 1:27–28).

And such was God's intention with the reluctant and stammering Moses. Through this ill-suited and recalcitrant individual, God led his chosen people out of bondage into the promised land, and the program of salvation went forward. It wasn't without its challenges, of course. Moses still pleaded to be excused, and for the first time in the Bible it is said that "the Lord became angry." But God accommodated Moses' objections, appointing his brother, Aaron, as the spokesman, and Moses had nowhere else to turn. So, "Moses took his wife and children, mounted them on a donkey, and set out for Egypt" (4:20).

I wonder whether these words fall on any Moses-like ears? Many of us are at a time of personal discernment and discovery, and it is very easy for some of us to feel overwhelmed by our inadequacies. We may not possess the intellectual gifts to be at the top of the class. Or we may be aware of deficits in our people skills—clergy are generally known to be strong introverts! It may be that the prospect of leading others is daunting, especially at a time when the church is undergoing tumultuous change and experiencing rancor and conflict. And one can imagine that our insecurities and lack of confidence can be obstacles in our desire to hear God's call and respond in obedience. If this describes your situation, God may wish to say to you, "Who is it that gives man speech? Who makes him dumb or deaf? Who makes him keen-sighted or blind? Is it not I, the Lord? Go now; I shall help you to speak and show you what to say." The story we are a part of is not about us, it is about God. And we must be content to let God use us in our weakness to display his strength.

On the other hand, there may be others here who think that we have our calling cased. Confident in our skills and abilities, we are inclined to rely on our own strength and charisma, and we may indeed find "success" as the world understands the term. We also need to hear God ask, "Who is it that gives man speech?"—only for us, the answer comes not as an encouragement, but as a warning. We need to be reminded that the story is not about us, either. The great OT scholar Gerhard von Rad once wrote,

"Neither previous faith nor any other personal endowment have the slightest part to play in preparing [one] who was called to stand before Yahweh for his vocation." Our God-given capacities are wonderful things, and they find their proper place when bent to the purposes of God. But it is God's way to exploit weakness, and if there is any legacy, any monument fit for the kingdom, it will come as we, with Moses in the eyes of the writer to the Hebrews, consider "abuse suffered for Christ to be greater wealth than the treasures of Egypt" (Heb 11:26).

Scripture: Exodus 4:10–23

Questions for Further Reflection:

1. As you consider God's call on your own life, or on the life of your community, are there any particular weaknesses which you feel disqualify you from serving God?

2. In what ways might God be using these perceived weaknesses to demonstrate his own strength and sufficiency?

3. How does the gospel of Jesus Christ help you to reconsider these weaknesses?

5

From Bitterness to Joy
Lessons in the Wilderness School

Thomas Power

The general theme of the book of Exodus is the fulfillment of God's promise to Abraham to make his descendants into a great nation. It is the story of God's redemption of his people and of his drawing them into relationship. Of its forty chapters, the first eighteen recount the ways in which this redemption takes place: redemption from Egypt through the plagues; redemption from death through the Passover; redemption from destruction through the Red Sea; and redemption from the wilderness through God's provision. It is to this last aspect of redemption that these verses apply.

To set the scene, the Hebrews are feeling euphoric after being delivered from their Egyptian oppressors. They have a sense of the freedom and possibility that this deliverance has brought. This is evident in the preceding verses with the songs of Moses and Miriam celebrating God's act of rescue at the Red Sea. They are joyful and uplifted. Their disposition is summed up in Miriam's song, "Sing to the Lord, for he is highly exalted" (15:21). Physically they are liberated, having cast off the oppression of the Egyptians; but spiritually they are not yet liberated. Then things change quickly. After they cross the Red Sea, they stop in the wilderness because they are in need of water. But the only water to be had is bitter, so they complain. In response, God instructs Moses to throw a tree into the water, which is then made sweet. Then God gives them some instructions which, if they obey them, will result in God not bringing on them the destruction he brought on the Egyptians. They then go on to Elim where there is water aplenty.

On the surface, the meaning of these verses might appear deceptively simple. In fact, they reveal a pattern of divine purpose and human behavior that is to be repeated many times again. The passage is a microcosm of the entire wilderness experience: basic human needs and the struggle to obey God. If we are to learn something from this passage, it is important to note its sequence and progression.

Thirsting for water is their first need. Although Egypt had been a land of oppression, for the Hebrews it had also been a land of plenty with water in abundance. Then, after they are freed through the crossing of the Red Sea, everything changes. After the high point has passed and the songs of praise sung, the mood of the people shifts and they face their first crisis. As they journey through the desert they find their supply of water has run out. They seek it but it cannot be found. For three days they travel in the desert without finding water. Then, when they arrive at a place that has water, they find it is bitter. They are unable to grasp that the God who could perform what looked like the impossible task of getting them through the Red Sea could also perform a lesser task of providing them with water for their sustenance. They do not understand this. Could they not realize that the God who was powerful enough to raise the Red Sea for them to pass through, could also perform a lesser task and supply them with water to drink?

Is that not all too often our attitude too? We look to God to deliver us from the impossible difficulties that assail us, and then forget that his provision does not end there, but that God also supplies our lesser but perhaps more essential needs. In other words, part of faith and trust is to realize that God is intimately concerned with all the minutiae of our lives. This tells us something about the nature of God: God is one who acts and provides, even in the small but essential things. In all this God's desire is for us to seek him and be dependent on him alone, the source of living water. It is about *need* leading to relationship.

Secondly, unfulfilled need leads to grumbling and discontent, just as in some of the Psalms. Instead of recognizing and trusting in God to deliver their every need, they grumble against Moses, saying "What are we to drink?" They are hopeful as they see a pool ahead, only to be disappointed when they find it is too bitter to drink. So if their first experience was the need for water, their second was disappointment when they found it, because it was bitter, the meaning of Marah. Not only was Marah a reminder of the bitter experiences in Egypt and of the bitter herbs used at Passover, but it represents a place of disappointment, failure, dashed hopes and expectations, and brokenness.

Thirdly, there is intercession. Moses brings their complaint before God, and in response God instructs him to toss the wood into the water, which he does obediently and it makes it sweet. Moses does what God commands, but without understanding why or how it is going to work, just as in earlier situations. He obeys and this obedience leads to blessing and healing.

So we have need, complaint, occasioning intercession. Fourthly, and relatedly, there is divine response and action. God responds to Moses' appeal; God performs a miracle. The result is that the water becomes sweet and the people's need is met.

Meeting their need becomes the occasion for God to teach them something of himself. To do so, God vows that the provision made for them will be repeated if they obey God's law. So the miracle is accompanied by the giving of rules for living in relationship, implying that rules are essential for a life-giving relationship to thrive. What are the rules God lays down? The people are cautioned to listen to God's words, as Moses instructs them ("If you listen carefully to the voice of the Lord your God and do what is right in his eyes"), but not only to listen ("If you pay attention to his commands"), and finally, not only to listen and pay attention but "[to] keep all his decrees." If these conditions of listening, attentiveness, and observance are present, then God promises, "I will not bring on you any of the diseases I brought on the Egyptians, for I am the Lord who heals you" (v. 26). If we need to be reminded what obedience to God entails, it is clearly stated here. All these things are attributes of obedience: listening, paying attention, and keeping or observing. Obedience is made the basis of relationship. To obey God is to know God.

Finally, God provides for them again, this time abundantly as God brings them to Elim. This is a place with twelve springs of water and seventy palm trees. Elim with abundant water is further evidence of God's prodigious care.

What does all this mean for us? If we are to find ourselves in this story, it involves us seeing that we have all left something behind in order to embark on the journey of faith. We have abandoned our Egypt, represented in a former state, whether of the oppressiveness of sin, unbelief, allegiances, or idolatries. We are now in a wilderness, poised between Marah and Elim. Marah—representing death, sin, despair—is at one extreme, and at the other is Elim—representing life, redemption, and resurrection. In between is that piece of wood tossed into the water, likely a porous log capable of absorbing its impurities, just as Jesus on the wooden cross absorbed all our sin and cleansed us. We cannot proceed to Elim without going through the Cross. On that journey, God provides us with the rules and practices that deepen relationship through obedience. In answer to the question posed by the people to Moses—"What are we to drink?"—we can affirm the words of Jesus, "If any thirst, let him come to me and drink" (John 7:37).

Scripture: Exodus 15:23–27

Questions for Further Reflection:

1. Earlier in the book of Exodus, we are told that the Israelites had cried out to God from the midst of their captivity and that God had responded to their cry by calling Moses to lead them out of Egypt. How was their "crying out" at that time different than their "crying out" in our passage?

2. Thinking back on your own life, can you remember times in which God provided for your needs? How do these previous gifts of provision affect your present trust in God?

3. This essay challenges us to consider the story in a spiritual sense, by thinking of God's provision of the wood as the wood of the Cross, and the journey of the

Redemption and Relationship

Israelites out of Egypt as our own journey from unbelief to faith. As we know, the life of faith does not go back to one turning point (conversion), but time and again we are called to bring our sins and idolatries to the Cross, that we may continue our lives in Christ's resurrection. What "bitter" areas of your life need to be sweetened by the Cross?

6

This is the Word of the Lord

Catherine Sider-Hamilton

The Israelites said to Moses and Aaron, "If only we had died by the hand of the Lord in the land of Egypt, when we sat by the fleshpots and ate our fill of bread" (Exod 16:3). There is so little distance between God's good gift and the people's complaint. Right at the root of the life of God's people, there is a failure to trust God's word and to heed. Standing on the freedom side of the Red Sea, just a few verses earlier, the people have sung thanksgiving to their Lord: "I will sing to the Lord, for he has triumphed gloriously; / Horse and rider he has thrown into the sea. / The Lord is my strength and my might, /and he has become my salvation" (15:1–2). God has delivered his people from bondage in Egypt; he has snatched them right out from under the wheels of Pharaoh's chariots and made them walk on dry land through the sea. In the exodus, God has shown himself to be irreducibly, incontrovertibly for his people. This wilderness in which they now stand is the place of God's grace. "Sing to the Lord for he has triumphed gloriously," Miriam says (15:21). Yet eight short verses later the people say, "You have brought us out into this wilderness to kill us with hunger" (16:3).

In this, the swift turn from joy to accusation, from faith to fear, the Israelites are not particularly original. This has happened before in the history of God's people. It has happened in the garden at the beginning of the world. In Genesis 2 the Lord God puts the man in the garden he has planted and the Lord God makes to grow in the garden every tree that is pleasant to the sight and good for food, and he forms every beast of the field and every bird of the air. He makes from the man's rib a woman, and brings her to the man. And the man says, "This at last is bone of my bones and flesh of my flesh" (Gen 2:23). At last! You have given me, Lord, this one to whom I can cleave, this good gift. But just a few verses later, after the serpent and the fruit, the man will say, "The woman whom you gave me to be with me, she gave me the fruit of the tree, and I ate" (3:12). This woman *you* gave me, it's all her fault. It does not take long to go from joy in the gift God has given to bitter complaint at that very gift.

On the surface these are quite different stories. In Eden, the taking of the forbidden fruit, in the midst of so much plenty, taking the one fruit God has told them not to eat. In the wilderness of the Exodus there is no fruit and no taking. Here there is only hunger, desert, and fear, the felt absence of the Providence of God. And yet this moment in the wilderness is like that other moment in the garden. For the problem in both is a failure to hear the Word of God and to trust in it, to know that it is good. "Of every tree in the garden you may freely eat, but of the tree of the knowledge of good and evil you shall not eat, for in the day that you eat of it you shall die" (Gen 2:16–17). The word of God to the man and the woman in the garden is God's good gift. See, I set before you today life and death (Deut 30:15), every tree of the garden for food; only do not eat of the tree of the knowledge of good and evil, for it is death to you. God's word is from the beginning given to the people for life, and from the beginning the people do not heed the Word. Perhaps, they think, the serpent knows better. The problem in Eden is disobedience, the failure to heed God's word.

So, too, in Exodus. The fear of the people in the face of the wilderness—why did you bring us out here to kill us with hunger—this fear is also a failure of obedience. It is a failure to hear God's word, to hear and to heed, to know that God's word is constant and that God's word is good. Exodus frames the episode of the Israelites' complaint with God's commandment. "There the Lord made for them a statute and an ordinance" (15:25) the text says, immediately before this passage. "If you will listen carefully to the voice of the Lord your God and do what is right in his sight and give heed to his commandments and keep all his statutes, I will not bring upon you any of the diseases that I brought upon the Egyptians. For I am the Lord who heals you" (15:26). Immediately after this passage, Moses says, "It is the bread that the Lord has given you to eat. This is what the Lord has commanded: Gather as much as each of you needs," and do not store it up for the next day (16:15–16).

The freedom on the other side of the Red Sea comes, like the bounty of the garden, with God's commandment. God gives his people bread in the wilderness as God has given the people fruit, a garden out of chaos, in the first days of the world. God is the God of grace. But this grace— the fruit in the garden, the bread in the wilderness, the freedom on the other side of the Red Sea—all this grace comes with God's commandment. *Listen carefully to the voice of the Lord your God and do what is right in his sight. This is the bread the Lord has given you to eat: do not store it up for the next day.* Bread in the desert, God's gift of life, is not separable from the word of God, his commandment.

In the desert the people, of course, do not listen. They do not trust God's word; they do store up the food; and stored up, it is rotten, full of worms. In Exodus and in Eden, in the wilderness and in the garden, the problem in the lives of the people of God is the same. They do not heed the Word of God; they do not know that the Word of God is good. They think—we think—again and again that we know better. Fresh from the Red Sea the people accuse God, and make their own provisions.

In this God's people suffer a great loss. For the Word of God is meant for life. In the garden, in the wilderness, and in the church, the Word of God is meant for life. The commandment is precisely the providence of God. Do not eat of the tree of the knowledge of good and evil, for it is death to you. Do not store up the bread . . . because you do not need to. For God is the one who is with you to save. God himself will provide the bread that his people need, day after day. The Lord said to Moses, "I have seen the misery of my people who are in Egypt; I have heard their cry. I know their sufferings, and I have come down to deliver them" (Exod 3:7–8). God's people think that they stand in the wilderness alone. But the Lord God of hosts is their God, and they are his people, and He prepares a table before them, even in the desert a feast. *I will give you the bread that you need*, the Lord God says to his people. *It will rain down from heaven upon the earth. I will give you the bread that you need, and you will eat and be satisfied.* This is the Word of the Lord.

God's commandment to his people in the wilderness, like his commandment to humankind in the garden, is the word of promise: *I am your God, the God who has made you. Listen to my Word, because in it I am with you to save. I am with you in the Red Sea joy and I am with you in the wilderness where you cannot see my face. Trust me. Turn to me. Look to my word.* Do not look to your own provision, the words that you prefer—for they breed worms and rottenness. There is a greater gift here. *Look to my word*, the Lord God says in the garden and in the wilderness, *for I am with you and I am the one who saves.* Obedience—a cleaving to the word of God as Adam cleaved to his wife, a cleaving to the word of God till it is bone of my bones—obedience is the footpath to fullness of life.

For the bread in the wilderness, sign and pledge of God's saving word to a people who do not trust in that word, this bread does not stand alone. It points forward to that other bread, that other word of God's love for the people who accuse Him. For God so loved the world that he gave his only Son. When the world does not know him, when the world does not hear him, when the world stands by its own choice in the darkness alone, God gives his only Son. And he says, "This is my Son, the beloved. Listen to him" (Matt 17:5). *Listen to him for he is my Word. Hear in his word my love, your hope.* All the days of slavery, all the wilderness places, covered over in him by grace.

We know, this day, the wilderness and the feel of ashes on our foreheads. We know Adam's death and our own exile, our repeated solipsistic shattering of the garden. Even in our church, this place of God's grace, we know it today. Ashes and shattering, the failure to obey. But this day we know too the promise. God so loved the world. God so loved the world that he gave his only-begotten Son. There is bread in the wilderness of our turning away. God is with us, even here, in Jesus Christ our Lord. God is with us to save. This is the Word of the Lord.

But it is necessary to listen to him. It is necessary to trust and to obey. We have seen God's glory, glory as of the only-begotten Son, full of grace and truth. God shows us the way, life, grace, and peace in the one who is his Word. He gives us all his love. He asks only that we hear and heed, that we cleave to him. Bone of my bones, this Word of God's love, written in the Scriptures, known in Jesus Christ. And shall we then turn away? Shall we choose ashes and worms and the flaming sword, God's people cast out from the garden of grace?

See, I have set before you today life and death. Choose life, that you may live.

Scripture: Exodus 16:1–15

Questions for Further Reflection:

1. The sermon discusses the Israelites' complaining in the wilderness against the background of Adam and Eve's refusal to heed God's word in the Garden of Eden. Read Genesis 2:15—3:24 together with Exodus 16:1–15 (and its immediate context, Exod 15:25b–26, Exod 16:16–21). Note common themes of food and commandment and disobedience. What is the role of commandment in God's relation with his people in each passage?

2. Note Exodus 16:4. Why do you think God says that he sends the bread from heaven to test the people?

3. In John's Gospel, Jesus is "Word" (John 1:1–14) and "bread from heaven" (John 6:31–59), as in Exodus 16 bread from heaven comes with God's commandment. What does it mean that Jesus is both? For Jesus? For us? Read (for example) John 4:31–34; John 6:1–11, John 8:42–47; John 12:46–50; John 14:15–24; John 15:9–14.

4. What is the relation between love and obedience, for Jesus? for Israel? for us? What does it mean for God's people to live in love?

7

Ours is the Battle, Christ is the Victory

J. Glen Taylor

THE PASSAGE BEFORE US—THE story of Aaron and Hur upholding Moses' hands on the mount so that Joshua could successfully defeat the Amalekites—is well known and colorful. But what does the story mean for us today? That question can usually be answered by looking at the broader context.

As it turns out, we need look no farther than chapter 18 verse 8, which says, "Moses told . . . about all the hardships they [the Israelites] had met along the way and how the Lord had saved them." Here we can aptly infer an implied meaning for our narrative and others that deal with Israel's hard journey since crossing the Sea. These stories serve to recount *various ways in which God provides help along the desert journey between the point of salvation and the point of rest.* What I have put in italics could in fact be the title of a whole series of sermons on this broader section into which our story falls, namely 15:22–18:27. This is not only because of 18:8, but also 18:10 where Jethro affirms this, adding: "Now I know that the Lord is greater than all gods, for he did this to those who treated Israel arrogantly." Here a strongly theocentric *to God be the glory* tone is sounded, consistent with what we see in chapters 1-12.

In short, I see our biblical writer telling stories in chapters 16–18 that cohere nicely as a whole series of sermons under the following propositional title: *The Desert Journey between the Place of Salvation and the Place of Rest: How God for His Glory Provides Help Along the Way.* A breakdown of sermons on the various episodes that fall within the series could be as follows:

1. Celebrating God's Victories (15:20–21)—where women and prophets share Moses' leadership in the worship of a triumphant God

2. Bitter Water: *A Complaining Congregation* (15:22–27)—where God sweetened the water and provided them a lesson on the importance of obedience

3. No Food: *A Complaining Accusatory Congregation* (16:1–36)—where God, hearing the people's complaint, gloriously provides them with bread and meat, while underscoring the importance of adherence to his law

4. No Water: *A Testing Accusatory Congregation* (17:1–7)—where God, hearing Moses complaint about the complainants, graciously provides water from the rock

5. Enemy Invasion! (17:8–16)—where Israel fights back and where Aaron and Hur support Moses' intercession before a God who brings victory

6. Sharing Moses' Ministry (18:1–27)—where God's glory is remembered and where Jethro advised Moses to delegate responsibility

The first and sixth segments provide an envelope structure marked by a similar theme: Moses sharing leadership (the first with Miriam, his sister, and also a prophet, and the second—six in the list above—with appointed judges over the people). Between these lie four episodes in which there is a problem. Three involve a problem that leads to complaining—first about water quality, second about the lack of food, and third about the lack of water. Our episode, listed as five above, adds the problem of *attacking from without*—by the Amalekites—to the three responses just noted of *grumbling from within*. Each episode—most importantly—features a glorious God who fosters obedience to his good laws and who meets these challenges with patience, provision, and principled pedagogy while at the same time fostering the leadership of Moses and others.

With a God like that, why would any people quarrel and complain along the desert journey? Biblical commentator Peter Enns puts it well when he writes of the three episodes prior to ours:

> [T]hese three rapid-fire stories of rebellion in the desert stagger the imagination. Perhaps they are meant to. No sooner do the Israelites leave Egypt under the most miraculous of circumstances than they, within one month of their departure, lapse into an old pattern. *They again use their own perception of their circumstances as the standard by which to base reality.*[1]

God's people today are equally prone to let their circumstances be the basis for their outlook. Like the Israelites, we have failed to learn a vital truth about God. Here again is Enns:

---

1. Enns, *The Book of Exodus*, 321–22 (emphasis mine).

> They [the Israelites] still have not learned that *even though they are in a desert with no food or water, God is above the circumstances.* So they grumble. But God uses their grumbling as an occasion not to punish his people, but to teach them something about himself.[2]

If I were to conduct a survey that asked, "Have you gone through a dark period after your initial encounter with Christ?" many people would likely respond: "Absolutely." They might continue as follows: "When I first became a Christian I was keen, I could see God's hand everywhere, but over time I began to doubt. I became discontent and found myself criticizing those in the church, especially its leaders." At times it seems as if there is a whole segment of the Christian population that regards their contribution to the church to *do nothing* more than to point out the deficiencies in what others *actually do*.

But in the midst of each of these situations, there is an element of grace that comes in. Behind the scenes—and in ways that are less dramatic than rescue by crossing a sea on dry ground—God provided his people, as well as his chosen leader Moses (and others) with what they needed. God responded graciously to the demands of the people, while at the same time fostering their growth through "testing" their obedience to the principled precepts (such as resting on the Sabbath) that reflect his character. So bitter water is made sweeter, bread, meat, and sweet manna are added to the menu, and water is demonstrably supplied from the dry rock.

Christian leaders, take note where you fit into this passage. Unfortunately, like Moses, you are sitting ducks for criticism, grumbling, accusations, and people's

---

2. Ibid., 322 (emphasis mine).

projected anger against God. Any church leader who has not yet encountered what Moses did at the hands of faithless malcontents within a congregation need only wait; it will happen. One of my seminary professors gave good advice when he urged three qualifications on prospective leaders of Christian congregations: 1) be called by God, 2) have the heart of a lion, and 3) have the hide of a rhinoceros! It takes a grace filled heart as well as a thick skin to cope with a congregation that gripes. Note as well, that criticism and complaining doesn't necessarily mean that a Christian leader is ineffective or wrong-headed. On the contrary, opposition often comes with the territory. This makes it all the more important for leaders to heed the implication of cases one and six above, namely to share the responsibilities of leadership with others who are qualified and similarly called. Fortunately, although it is true that congregations can wear down their leaders, there is Good News. We have seen much of it already in the character of a responsive, patient, morally principled God. But there is more. Like Moses, we Christian leaders can bring all of our concerns before God, whose ministry after all it truly is (not ours). And, by God's enabling grace, we are called to emulate the patience, attentiveness, and grace of God that is portrayed in these passages.

What then of the problem that arose in our episode from outside the congregation? In other words, what is the significance of the reference to Amalek attacking Israel in verse 8? This is the first instance since God's victory over Pharaoh that warfare is mentioned. (Warfare for the covenant community does not end with the defeat of the principle tyrant.) First appearing just after the promise given to Abram in Genesis 12, and involved in a battle that includes Abram in Genesis 14, the Amalekites typify the sort of enemy whose persistence, ruthlessness, and determination to destroy makes their continued survival an ever-present threat. Recalling Israel's encounters with the Amalekites in the wilderness, Moses writes:

> Remember what the Amalekites did to you long ago on the way when you came out of Egypt? When you were weary and worn out they met you on your journey and cut off all who were lagging behind. They had no fear of God. When the Lord your God gives you rest from all the enemies around you in the land he is giving you to possess as an inheritance, you shall blot out the memory of Amalek from under Heaven. Do not forget (Deut 25:15-17).

And how does God provide in the case of an attack on God's people by so notorious an enemy? At least in the present case (which, being memorialized, implies the need for continued resolve to defeat the Amalekites), the strategy involved a hard thing: fighting back (Exod 17:9). As the Book of Ecclesiastes reminds us, there is a time to fight. And this was one of them; the Amalekites were later to discourage Israelite spies from taking the Promised Land, even later to oppose Davidic kingship through which the Messiah was promised, and still later (through Haman in the Book of Esther) to attempt to annihilate the Jewish people. Esther's response to the Amalekite threat was clear (though troubling): to fight back hard.

How should this call to engage in warfare against human enemies of God's people be applied today, if at all? And, if so, who or what today might qualify as Amalekite? That is a difficult question, but it need not detract us from recognizing that the people of God can (and sometimes do) face mortal enemies today. It is naïve and dangerous to believe otherwise. As important as the battle was, the focus of the story lies elsewhere. It lies with what Moses did on the hill as he held the symbol of God's victory: he raised his hands to God as he stood "on the mountain" (reminiscent of Sinai to come). By shining the spotlight on the support that Aaron and Hur gave to Moses by "propping up" his hands, the writer emphasizes the support that Aaron and Hur gave Moses as he in turn interceded for those engaged in battle. In its historical context, the picture was that of "upholding" as a possible explanation for the place name Rephidim (a meaning which is attested in Arabic *rafada* and elsewhere as "holding up"); in its historical context too, the picture was also that of God working through the generation to follow Moses (Joshua and Hur) as well as that of speaking to future generations through the memorial of the book and the altar in vv. 14–16 (i.e., that God is committed to defeating the Amalekite enemy).

But the meaning of the support given by Aaron and Hur to Moses goes farther than that. It includes a marvelous picture of cooperation and support for the mission of intercession before God, a mission that functioned in tandem with actual engagement (also involving cooperation and support) in battle. And at the level of typology, it also includes Moses as a type of Christ. This is so in at least two ways. First, Christ clearly fulfilled the prophecy in Deuteronomy of a prophet like Moses who would come (18:15-18). Second, Moses has often been interpreted in this passage as a type of Christ, whose arms were outstretched on a hill with a human on one side and another on the other, as at Calvary. And third, relative to the preceding episode in 17:17 in which the Lord appeared in front of Moses who held the staff, it is striking that Moses appears alone here, without the Lord. Perhaps Moses functions in the place of the Lord, the combined effect of which is to typify Jesus as both the new Moses and the Lord himself. These typological allusions are suggestive of an intercessory role that Christ plays for us.

As the Book of Hebrews reminds us, Jesus, our great High Priest intercedes for us. So, along with the historic picture of Moses, there also on the hill, allowing us to minister at his side and in a supportive role, stands our Lord with his arms outstretched—the God-man, the Moses-Christ—interceding for us. And so long as he intercedes for us, there is hope. During those dry desert periods that lie between past redemption and future rest there will be challenges, one being the grumbling of God's people before their leaders. But take heart; we have a God who listens and intercedes. Ours is the battle; Christ's is the victory. Or, even better, ours is the battle; Christ (alone) is the victory.

Scripture: Exodus 18:1–27

Questions for Further Reflection:

1. Does your experience of life with God have any parallels with the Israelites? Have you gone through a dark period after your initial encounter with Christ? What did you learn from that experience?

2. Whom do you identify with in the passage? What lessons can you draw away by placing yourself in the story?

8

God's Gift of Days and Life

Annette Brownlee

Exodus 19 marks a sharp break with what has proceeded it. The goal of the journey from Egypt has been reached. It is the third new moon (three months) since the people have fled through the Red Sea. During that time, God has sustained them: given them bread, quail, water and protection from the Amalekites. Now, they have arrived in the wilderness of Sinai. They have stopped and camped at the foot of the mountain. The goal of the journey from Egypt has been reached. What is that goal? God has brought them to himself. Is not that a beautiful description of the purpose of all this? God bore them on eagles' wings and has brought them to himself. In the beginning of chapter nineteen God announces to Moses the purpose of bringing the people to himself (19:3–6):

> Then Moses went up to God; the LORD called to him from the mountain, saying, "Thus you shall say to the house of Jacob, and tell the Israelites: You have seen what I did to the Egyptians, and how I bore you on eagles' wings and brought you to myself. Now therefore, if you obey my voice

> and keep my covenant, you shall be my treasured possession out of all the peoples. Indeed, the whole earth is mine, but you shall be for me a priestly kingdom and a holy nation. These are the words that you shall speak to the Israelites."

Moses speaks these words to the people. Before hearing any details, the people respond with one voice, "Everything the Lord has spoken we will do" (19:8). This seems a bit like signing one's name to a contract—or clicking the "I accept" button—before we read the fine print we have been instructed to read. But to a person Israel signs on. "Everything the Lord has spoken we will do." The rabbinic literature on this verse focuses on the fact that 100 percent of the people signed on. If one person had not gone along, they would not have been worthy of receiving the *Torah*. Their acceptance to the person is only a first step. There is much more to come; and God instructs Moses to have the people consecrate themselves for two days to prepare for what will happen on the third. God, as it turns out, is not at the end of a remote. God tells them what to do: wash your clothes, stay away from the sacred area around the mountain, and separate yourself from what is normally permitted and good. Finally, when the trumpet or *shofar* sounds a long, loud blast, go up the mountain.

The second half of chapter nineteen contains what is called a theophany. A theophany is a specular manifestation of God which humans can apprehend. Only after that does God speak the words we know as the Decalogue, the Ten Words or Ten Commandments. It is the contrast between the two I want to point out. The contrast helps us to receive the gift of God's covenant with Israel, which we have been grafted into through Jesus Christ. And perhaps, it helps us to direct our eyes to the Giver of that gift.

The theophany is as spectacular as it is terrifying. On the third day a thick cloud descends on the mountain with lightning and thunder, the promised loud horn, then fire and smoke and the whole mountain shakes. There is confusion, Moses running back up the mountain, Aaron getting involved. The people tremble and are terrified; and given this display, how could their response be anything but that? And then God speaks, not in thunder, but in *words*. After the smoke, fire, volcano, earthquake, confusion, thunder, lightning, and loud horns, God speaks ordinary words. Quite prosaic, actually: honor your mother and father; do not steal; keep the Sabbath; do not have idols; worship only God; do not covet your neighbor's donkeys. Donkeys? After such a spectacular display of God as Creator, God is now talking to us about our parents, and our neighbor's donkeys? After parting the Red Sea, killing Pharaoh's army, bearing us on eagles' wings, raining down quail and manna, giving us water and protection, terrifying us on the mountain—all this—to tell us not to covet our neighbor's donkey? Really? Yes.

The covenant God makes with Israel is not timebound, because God is not timebound, and God cannot be unfaithful to himself. "Though heaven and earth will pass away the Word of the Lord endures forever" (Matt 24:35). But God has made a covenant with Israel. That is, with a people: creatures who are timebound, who are fundamentally different than God in this and every respect. In the Law, God accommodates himself to this difference—that is, to his creatures. In the Law God clothes his covenant in the stuff of our lives, just as Jesus in the fullness of time will clothe himself in our flesh and fulfill the Law. In coming down to meet Moses on the mountain and give the Law, God descends to a place he does not belong: honor your mother and father; do not steal;

keep the Sabbath; do not have idols; worship only God; do not covet your neighbor's donkeys or anything else that belongs to your neighbor. The theophany, covenant, and Law together mark Israel's destiny in this world. God has set them apart and made them his holy possession. The Decalogue is the ordering of creaturely life toward the reality of what God has given them.

What God has given them—and what they have signed on for to a person—is a life within a people, with God and neighbor throughout generations. What God has given them—whether it is "at last, bone of my bone and flesh of my flesh," or manna, water, and protection, or a covenant and the Law—is all the same, really. The same in that what is given points back to the Giver, and the priority of God, who is beyond all these creaturely gifts, as the theophany reveals. And all that God gives is given for a single reason: to draw his people back to himself, just as he has drawn them through the Red Sea, and three moons in the wilderness, "to himself." Here, in the prosaic words of the Decalogue, God bears them not on eagles' wings, but on something sturdier for their long passage through time. The theophany, Law, and covenant belong together. The people's reaction to the theophany was terror—how could it not be? But God asks for more than emotion; God asks for obedience. The Decalogue guards against internalizing and spiritualizing our relationship with God and comes with judgement, for his covenant claims and defines creaturehood and demands full commitment on who we are, the purpose of life and death.

The poet Philip Larkin asks the question: what are days for? "Days are where we live," he writes. The Decalogue adds: days are where God lives with us. Days are where we learn that we are most fully human when we realize we are recipients—of God's gift of days, of God's gift of life. And God's gift of the Decalogue, for the ordering of that received life, towards God and neighbor, the full extent of the gift.

The Rabbinic literature on this section says that God offered the covenant to all the nations, but when they heard its content, all declined but Israel. I guess everyone but Israel actually read that fine print. And we know the shelf life of Israel's unanimous assent. But God's covenant is not time- or people-bound because God is not. In the fullness of time God draws his people back to himself, not only on eagles' wings and the Law, but on the outstretched arms of his son. For the way God has given for Israel to live with him is to be our way as well. Amen.

Scripture: Exodus 19:16—20:17

Questions for Further Reflection:

1. How does Exodus 19 set up a contrast between the theophany of God to Israel and the giving of the Ten Commandments to them?
2. In what ways is the giving of the Ten Commandments a gift to the people of Israel, and to us?

9

Moses' Intercession for Israel, and How It Helps Us Understand the Cross

ALAN L. HAYES

MOSES HAS GONE UP Mount Sinai to speak with God, and to receive the tablets of the law and the oral law. The people have remained below in the Sinai wilderness, waiting. The days go by, and the people begin to wonder when Moses is going to be coming back. "We do not know what has become of him," they say (Exod 32:1). And the mood of the people begins to change, though the text does not exactly say how or why. Maybe the people are beginning to feel the freedom that comes when firm authority has been removed, like kids in grade five when the substitute teacher comes. Maybe they are anxious about their future, and hope that creating a god will make them feel more secure. Maybe they are annoyed at Moses for leaving them, and one way to act out their annoyance is to rebel and do exactly what he has told them not to do. In any event, the people fashion a golden calf, and they worship it and offer sacrifice to it, in violation of the commandment against idolatry which Moses only recently has given them. The passage is interesting for a number of reasons that we will not explore here. It is a case study in how people behave when they are left to their own devices. It tells us something about the appeals of idolatry. It is also a wonderful example of very bad leadership, because the high priest Aaron enables the whole enterprise.

But let me draw your attention to something in the passage that is hugely important for how we understand God and Christ and Israel. After the people worship their golden calf, God tells Moses that he is so disgusted with this idolatry that he has determined to destroy Israel. God still wants to have a covenant people, though, so God declares that he will replace the house of Israel with the house of Moses. Not for a moment, however, does Moses consider allowing that option. In fact, a few verses after this passage, he says that if Israel is to be blotted out, he will insist on being blotted out with them. In other words, if Israel is not to be God's people, then *no people* will be God's people. Moses reminds God of the promise he made to Abraham, Isaac, and Jacob, to make of their descendants a great nation. And God indeed changes his mind.

In all the Old Testament, Moses' successful intercession with God to save his people is the most important type, or prefiguring, of Christ's intercession on the Cross, when he pleads with God, "Father, forgive them" (Luke 23:34). And this is more than an interesting literary observation, for it is essential to see the Cross in its Old Testament context.

Let me begin to get at that by telling a personal story, which I should warn you is a little dark. In 1957, I became a junior high school student. Of many things that changed that year, one was that I began to take physical education. Every day the boys went to the boys' gym where we put on our gym clothes, did whatever we did on a particular day—run a mile, do calisthenics, climb ropes, play soccer—then we took a shower in the big communal shower room, put on our street clothes, and went to our next class. That was the routine. But my friend Mike was not required to take a shower. Almost no one knew why. There was speculation. Was he shy? Did he have some terrible physical deformity under his clothes? Did he have an allergy to water? I will tell you the truth of it; Mike was Jewish. And from the time he had been very small, Mike had a recurrent nightmare several times a week where he was being herded with other young Jewish boys and girls, along with Jewish men and women of all ages, into a big shower room, and the doors were locked, and gas started coming out of the shower heads, and people began screaming and trying to claw their way out, and Mike would wake up, and he was screaming too, in a cold sweat. And in grade seven, when we all went to the boys' gym and saw the shower room for the first time, Mike could not go in there. He told Coach Johnson his story, and Coach said to him, "You won't ever have to take showers here." Mike, like me, was born a year after the death camps were closed, but his life was shaped by them.

In my puzzled eleven-year-old way, I began wondering why Jews were victims of history in a way that Christians were not, and I sensed that the answer might lie in the fact that my society was overwhelmingly Christian, and Jews were a tiny minority. Besides Mike, there were only a few Jews in my high school class, and I was friendly with most of them. But I began to be aware that many of my own Christian teachers and friends, and a lot of Christian society in general, did not like Jews. They marginalized them, and indeed often despised them as a group, calling them scallywags and shysters and subversives and even Christ-killers. Maybe more than any other single thing, although there were other things too, the disconnect between how so many Christians understood Jews and Judaism, and my own experience of Jews and Judaism, made me question everything my church taught me.

One particular confusion that I found it hard to sort out was that everyone seemed to recognize that Jesus was Jewish, but the Christianity that I was aware of did not really picture him that way. Our sermons and our Sunday school teaching and our Christian theology portrayed Jesus as a kind of honorary Gentile, either free of ethnicity, or else a free-thinking Jew who opposed the errors of Judaism. When I was still in junior high school, an outrageously pretty Jewish girl named Liz was chosen by our Sunday school Christmas pageant committee to play the part of the Blessed Virgin Mary. Many objected, but my parents laughed and said that finally the church had got it right. But the Jesus that I saw in the pictures in my Bible, and in the stained-glass windows, did not look like a son that Liz Mandelson could ever have borne. Throughout the years that I was growing up, the picture of Jesus that everyone knew was Warner Sallman's head of Christ, the most influential devotional portrait of Jesus in history. It has been reproduced over half a billion times. You saw it everywhere as the definitive portrait of Jesus. And the "Sallman" Christ had white skin, blue eyes, and flowing brown hair. When Campus Crusade produced the film *Jesus* in 1979, they did not want an actor who looked Jewish; they wanted an actor who looked like Warner Sallman's Christ.

The way mainstream Christian theology ignored the Jewishness of Jesus started the church down the road to the Holocaust. It turns out that theology is not irrelevant stuff about angels dancing on the head of a pin. Theology is a life and death matter, and for millions of Jews it has been a death matter. The church began de-Judaizing Christ within a few decades of the Resurrection. As Christianity became predominantly Gentile, theologians did not want to showcase the ethnic identity of Jesus, because that wasn't a basis on which Gentiles could identify with him. The basis on which they could identify with Jesus was simply that, like Jesus, they were human beings. And so in none of the usual doctrines of the atonement, whether Anselm or Abelard or *Christus Victor*, does it matter that Jesus was a Jew. But in the New Testament, it does matter that when God came to dwell among us, he was a historical human being in a specific time and place, thoroughly Jewish in ancestry and culture and ethnicity.

Jesus' Jewishness was crucial because the Bible says that salvation comes from Israel. Mainstream Christianity before the 1950s tried to get around that embarrassment by teaching that God had rejected the Israel of the Old Testament and replaced it with the church. This mainstream Christian theology of a de-Judaized Jesus and a rejected Israel, taken to an extreme, became the Nazi theology that justified the Holocaust and created my friend Mike's nightmares. Yes, there were some German theologians, like Barth and Bonhoeffer, who fought against the error of a de-Judaized Jesus, but they were scarcely heard at the time, though they certainly are heard now. The Nazis created a new Bible that had no Old Testament, and that reduced the New Testament sixty percent by eliminating every obvious reference to Judaism unless it was negative. The genealogy in Matthew was the first to go. Jesus was preached by the Nazi church as a person of Aryan race—that is, white race—who hated Jews and who therefore roused the hatred of the Jews and who was killed as a result. The Nazi church, therefore, thought it was being faithful by trying

Redemption and Relationship

to get rid of Jews. On Kristallnacht in November 1938, the German mobs smashed the synagogues and the shops owned by Jews, and burned the Torah scrolls; and then things kept getting worse. Nazi scholars justified the campaigns against the Jews; some of them remained influential long after the war—people like Gerhard Kittel, whose theological wordbook you may even have used, and Walter Grundmann, whose theological works were still standard texts in German seminaries as late as the 1990s.

After World War II, after the Holocaust, Christian leaders were struck in conscience to realize that the centuries of ignoring Jesus' Judaism had taken things so seriously and murderously wrong. In the seminaries and biblical guilds, a renewed respect for the Old Testament and biblical theology started to flourish. This movement had not touched my own church in the 1950s, since the leaders had not kept up with their continuing education! But in the decades since then, our appreciation of the Scriptures has been immeasurably enriched by seeing the Old Testament in the New.

And that brings us back to the picture in Exodus 32, where Moses stands before God, pleads with God to remember his promises and covenant, and persuades God to put away his wrath. This is not the first or the last time for such an image in the Old Testament, though it is the most important and most dramatic. The pattern in the Old Testament is that God's people sin, God threatens judgment, a representative of Israel who has been raised by God intercedes, and God is merciful. Abraham pleads with God to turn away his wrath from Sodom. True, the results there are mixed. Samuel twice prays to God in repentance and makes an offering in intercession for Israel. Twice Amos receives a vision of God's destruction of Israel; twice he pleads for

God's forgiveness and mercy; twice God turns away his wrath. Jeremiah dares to intercede for a people that are impenitent, to a God who is determined to punish; and Jeremiah, like Jesus, speaks both for Israel and for God. In the fourth Servant Song of Isaiah, the Servant intercedes with God, bears the sin of the people, suffers, and dies.

Jesus thinks of himself in the same line of atoning intercession. Listen to the parable that he tells on the way to the Cross. Imagine an orchard, he says, with an unfruitful fig tree—and we know that the fig tree is a common symbol for Israel. The owner of the orchard tells his gardener to uproot the offending fig tree. But the gardener pleads for it, intercedes for it, makes atonement for it, not because the fig tree is deserving, but because it bears a promise of fruitfulness, and the gardener himself will do his best to make it fruitful. The gardener is Christ, turning God's wrath from the fig tree, and, with his own blood, making the fig tree to flourish again.

So when we think of the Cross of Christ, we can understand its significance best if we remember Moses on Mount Sinai, pleading for Israel before God. As Moses knew, there is no other people that can take the place of Israel; there can be no question of rejecting Israel and starting over. God is faithful to his promises. Jesus is nailed to the Cross not as a generic human being, but as the descendant of King David, and the Messiah of Israel's God; he is identified on the Cross ironically but truly as the King of the Jews. His intercession with God for Israel—"Father, forgive them"—cannot be unsuccessful. In his last breath, as he says "It is finished" (John 19:30), he is also saying "It is fulfilled." God has remembered his promises and his covenant, and has forgiven Israel. The church has often seen Christ as the victim of the Jews, but the Bible celebrates

Christ as the Savior of the Jews. Christ's blood is the regeneration of Israel, the fulfillment of Israel's prophecies.

Our connection with Jesus is not simply that we are human beings and he was a human being, too. Our connection is that through our baptism we share in his death for the salvation of Israel, and by being grafted into Israel, we share in the promises that God made to Abraham, Isaac, and Jacob, the very promises that God remembered when he spoke to Moses on Mount Sinai. For the good news is that Christ has brought us into God's people, intercedes for us still, and has made us the heirs of salvation. Thanks be to God!

Scripture: Exodus 32:1–14

Questions for Further Reflection:

1. When you picture Jesus, do you think of him as a Jewish rabbi? Or is it preferable to picture him without a specific ethnicity?

2. This scripture meditation alludes indirectly to St. Paul's idea, in Romans 9–11, that, through Christ, Gentiles (non-Jews) have been grafted into Israel like rose buds from one bush into the stock plant of another bush. Is that the best way to picture things, or is it better to think of Christianity and Judaism as quite separate? What difference do you think it makes?

3. Many Christians believe that the Cross of Christ is a really significant event in establishing a close relationship between God and the church. Do you agree with that perspective? If not, why not? If so, why does the Cross make so much difference?

10

The Full Exodus Story

Peter Robinson

I GREW UP AS the middle child of five with only seven years' difference from the oldest to the youngest. We were not the quietest children. Once or twice when we were in full swing—doing things that we should not have been doing—my father would walk into the room. We were often so intent on what we were doing that it would take a moment or two for us to notice that he was there. But when we did we would stop what we were doing, freeze in place with our eyes fixed upon my father. We all knew that we were doing something wrong. This is the image that comes to mind as Moses descends from the mountain. He comes upon the people of Israel in the midst of their raucous celebration. After sacrificing to their new idol, their chosen god, they sat down to eat and drink and then got up to party (which is perhaps a euphemism for other behavior). You can almost see their awareness of Moses' presence spreading like a wave over their celebration. They know that what they have been doing is wrong. Perhaps a few of them quickly pull their clothes back on while others shuffle in front of the golden calf hoping to hide the evidence, but it is too late; Moses has seen more than enough.

Moses turns to Aaron and says, "What have you done?" (Exod 32:21). And Aaron does what all leaders are tempted to do when we are caught red handed: he desperately tries to shift the blame. *Moses, we did not know if you were going to come back, and why did you take so long? Moses, you need to understand, the people made me do it. And the calf . . . well, that just happened, it appeared out of the fire all on its own.* Aaron's excuses get weaker and weaker as he digs himself deeper into the pit of deceit and blame. And that brings us to the place where this story is hard to read. In fact, the next part of this story is abhorrent to us; there is no easy way to understand this. Moses grinds up the golden calf, makes the people swallow their god, and then he sends the Levites through the camp with swords and three thousand people are killed—their own people, members of their own families. And if that were not enough, God sends a plague on the people.

Exodus 32–34 stands as the penultimate moment in the story of the people's escape out of Egypt. Over and over again they have met various challenges—Pharaoh, the Egyptian army, hunger, thirst, desperation—and every time God has provided. We are told that God has been testing them, which means he has been working to form in their hearts trust and confidence in who God is: that God is faithful, gracious, and generous. So much so that, even when their situations seem overwhelming, they could know and trust God. And now Moses descends with the commandments: God's law, God's gift to them, the work of God's hands, which is to guide them as to how they should live as God's people. This story is coming to its climax where the people will finally and fully be able to give themselves to God. That is the appropriate response to God's faithful care of saving, providing, guiding, and teaching them—all so that they will be able to trust him and put their confidence wholly in God. God has earned their trust. But that is not what happens. Instead, at this crucial moment in the story of God's shaping of this people, they reject God and then blame God for what has gone wrong: *God, if only you had acted more quickly, God if you had communicated more clearly, God we thought you had deserted us.* The tablets shattered at the foot of the mountain mirror the fracturing of the people's relationship with God. And the chapter ends with dire warnings of what is yet to come.

Their act of idolatry—creating a golden calf—is shocking not so much because they make an idol for themselves, as that they are declaring who they want God to be. Indeed, idolatry is not simply making idols; it is God's people turning their hearts and minds to something or someone other than God, all the while claiming that they are worshipping God. Idolatry is the deceit of believing that we get to choose who God is and that we get to discern what matters to God. Does that sound familiar?

We need to be careful not to try and offer a comprehensive explanation for the violence in this story. Yet we need to recognize this; this violence does not expose a character flaw in God. It does not suggest that this God, while claiming to be faithful, is actually capricious. No—if anything, this violence exposes the utter folly and destructive nature of the people's rejection of God and the devastating consequences of that rejection. What is particularly sobering is the recognition that in our churches today we have proven just as quick to seek other gods even while we claim to worship God. Money, power, influence: these are some of the gods we seek, and these gods are capricious.

It is the worship of these gods which leads to violence and destruction. In the light of our own unfaithfulness to God, we too should be left at the foot of the mountain with nothing more than the shattered tablets and the fractured relationship. Except that the exodus story doesn't end there.

In Jesus Christ we have the full story: God's word come down to us not simply as commandments written on stone, but the desires and hopes of God embodied in human flesh. And our violence is exposed for what it is: it is not primarily about God's violence against us, it is our violence against God. Jesus Christ, God with us, fractured and broken on the cross, silences our excuses, exposes our folly, and swallows the destructive results of our idolatry. On the cross Jesus reveals that to reject God, to act as though we get to choose who God is and what God is like, cannot help but bring utter chaos and destruction into our world. Yet Jesus reveals this not to condemn us but to deliver us. In Jesus Christ we are carried to the proper end of the exodus story. At the penultimate moment Jesus does not choose another God, he chooses to obey, to trust. He realizes the intended *telos* of the exodus story: human flesh made whole in its proper relationship with God. And where Moses once interceded for the people of Israel, Jesus intercedes for us. Seated at the right hand of the Father, he continues to intercede for us as the one who brings us to the true exodus so that we, without shame, can stand and look upon our heavenly Father.

Scripture: Exodus 32:15–35

Questions for Further Reflection:

1. Over and over again the story of Exodus relates God's faithfulness in providing for the people and how quickly they begin to doubt and despair. What causes doubt and despair to grow so quickly in our lives? How can we counter that doubt and despair?

2. How does the story of the Exodus out of Egypt provide a lens to understand what Jesus has done for us? How does Jesus' obedience contrast with the disobedience of the people of Israel?

3. What are some of the idols we struggle with in the church today?

Bibliography

Bible Gateway. "Jochebed." https://www.biblegateway.com/resources/all-women-bible/Jochebed.

Enns, Peter. *The Book of Exodus*. NIVAC. Grand Rapids: Zondervan, 2000.

Exum, Cheryl. "Second Thoughts about Secondary Characters: Women in Exodus 1:8—2:10." In *A Feminist Companion to Exodus to Deuteronomy*, edited by A. Brenner, 75–87. Sheffield: JSOT, 1994.

———. "'You Shall Let Every Daughter Live': A Study of Exodus 1:8—2:10." In *The Bible and Feminist Hermeneutics*, edited by M. A. Tolbert, 63–82. *Semeia* 28. Chico: Scholars, 1983.

Jenson, Robert. *Systematic Theology, Volume 1: The Triune God*. Oxford: Oxford University Press, 2001.

Lessing, Gotthold Ephraim. *Education of the Human Race*. London: Smith, 1858.

Sailhamer, John H. *The Pentateuch as Narrative: A Biblical-Theological Commentary*. Grand Rapids: Zondervan, 1992.

Seitz, Christopher R. *Word Without End: The Old Testament as Abiding Theological Witness*. Waco: Baylor University Press, 2004.

Trible, Phyllis. "Bringing Miriam Out of the Shadows." *Bible Review* 5 (1989) 16–24.

Whyte, Alexander. *Bible Characters: Adam to Achan*. London: Oliphant, 1896.

List of Contributors

Stephen G. W. Andrews
Principal of Wycliffe College

Annette Brownlee
Chaplain, Professor of Pastoral Theology, and Director of Field Education

Alan L. Hayes
Bishops Frederick and Heber Wilkinson Professor of Church History

L. Ann Jervis
Professor of New Testament

Thomas Power
Adjunct Professor of Church History, Theological Librarian

Ephraim Radner
Professor of Historical Theology

Peter Robinson
Professor of Proclamation, Worship, and Ministry

Catherine Sider-Hamilton
Professor of New Testament

J. Glen Taylor
Professor of Scripture and Global Christianity

List of Contributors

Marion Taylor
Professor of Old Testament

Andrew C. Witt
Recently received his PhD in Old Testament from Wycliffe College (University of St. Michael's College). He is the author of two journal articles, several book reviews, and an entry in the *Encyclopedia of the Bible and Its Reception*. As a Teaching Fellow and Adjunct Faculty at Wycliffe College, he has taught courses on the Psalms, an introduction to the Old Testament, and Introductory Biblical Hebrew.

www.ingramcontent.com/pod-product-compliance
Lightning Source LLC
Chambersburg PA
CBHW070059100426
42743CB00012B/2599